Go Green with Sesame Street

SAVE ENERGY, BERT AND ERNIE!

Jennifer Boothroyd

Lerner Publications ◆ Minneapolis

Cooperating and sharing are an important part of *Sesame Street*—and of taking care of our planet. We all share Earth, so it's up to all of us to take care of it together. The *Go Green with Sesame Street*® books cover everything from appreciating Earth's beauty, to conserving its resources, to helping keep it clean, and more. And the familiar, furry friends from *Sesame Street* offer young readers some easy ways to help protect their planet.

Sincerely,

The Editors at Sesame Workshop

The text of this book is printed on paper that is made with 30 percent recycled postconsumer waste fibers.

Table of Contents

Everyday Energy   **4**

Why Do We Need Energy?   **6**

Where Do We Get Energy?   **10**

How Can We Use Less Energy?   **18**

Earth Day Every Day   28
Have a Me-Powered Afternoon   30
Glossary   31
Index   32

Everyday Energy

Ernie, did you leave the TV on when you left the room?

I did, Bert. I guess I forgot to turn it off.

The TV uses energy. And energy is important, Ernie. Be careful not to waste it.

Why Do We Need Energy?

Energy helps us do so many things. It heats and cools our homes. Energy gives us light.

The microwave cooks my oatmeal quickly.

7

Energy helps us have fun.

It also helps us travel.

Energy makes cars go and airplanes fly.

Where Do We Get Energy?

Energy gives many things power.

A television uses electricity that comes from a cord.
A remote uses electricity from batteries.

I like watching people play *música* on television.

Factories make a lot of the energy we use.

Sometimes these factories make the air dirty.

The cleaner our air is, the healthier it is for people and animals.

Some ways of making energy
keep the air cleaner.

Solar energy comes
from the sun.

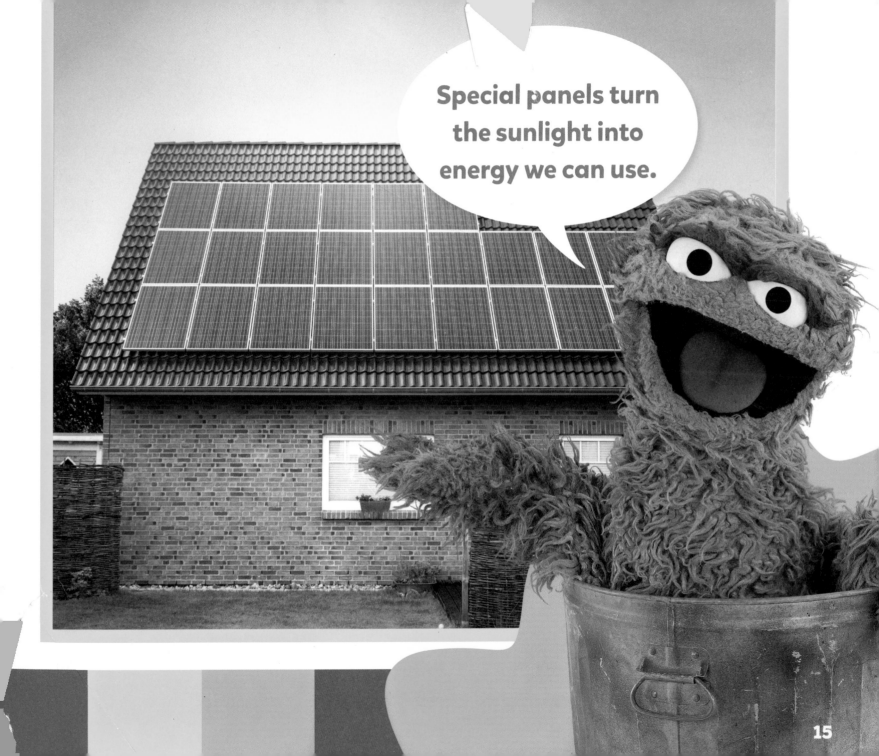

Wind spins the blades on a big windmill called a turbine. The turbine makes electricity. That's wind power!

Those turbines are huge.

They are even taller than me!

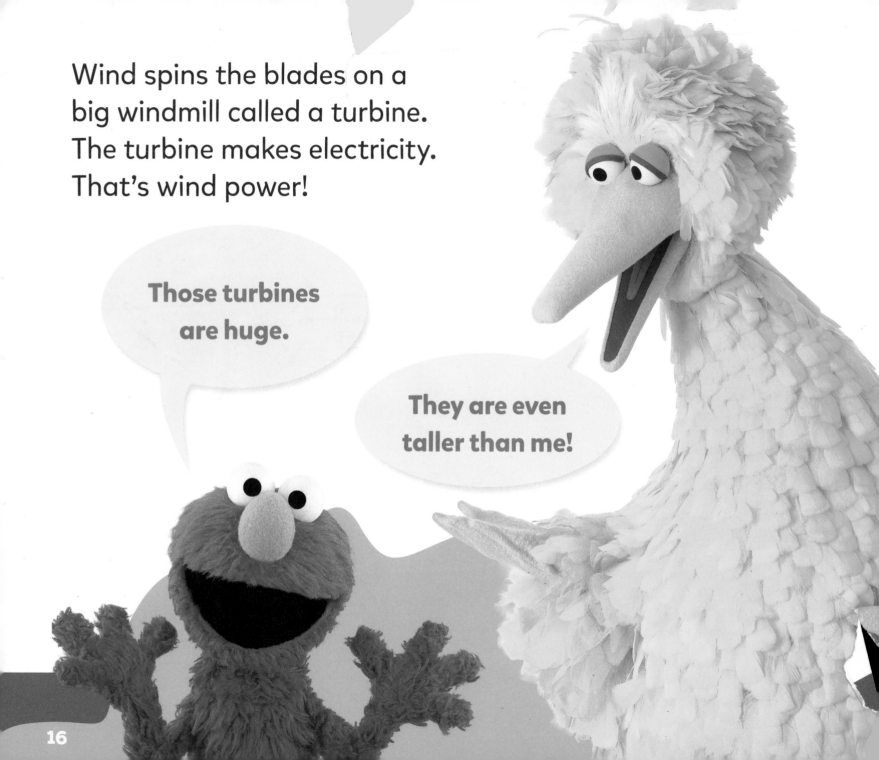

How Can We Use Less Energy?

Using less energy is a good way to keep the planet healthier.

When Earth is healthy, the people, plants, and animals that live on Earth can be healthy too!

There are many ways to use less energy. Always turn lights off when everyone leaves a room.

Sharing a car when you are on the go saves energy.

It's fun to carpool.

Walking or riding a bike uses your body's energy.

There are lots of ways to have fun without using electricity.

Build with blocks! Make a fort!

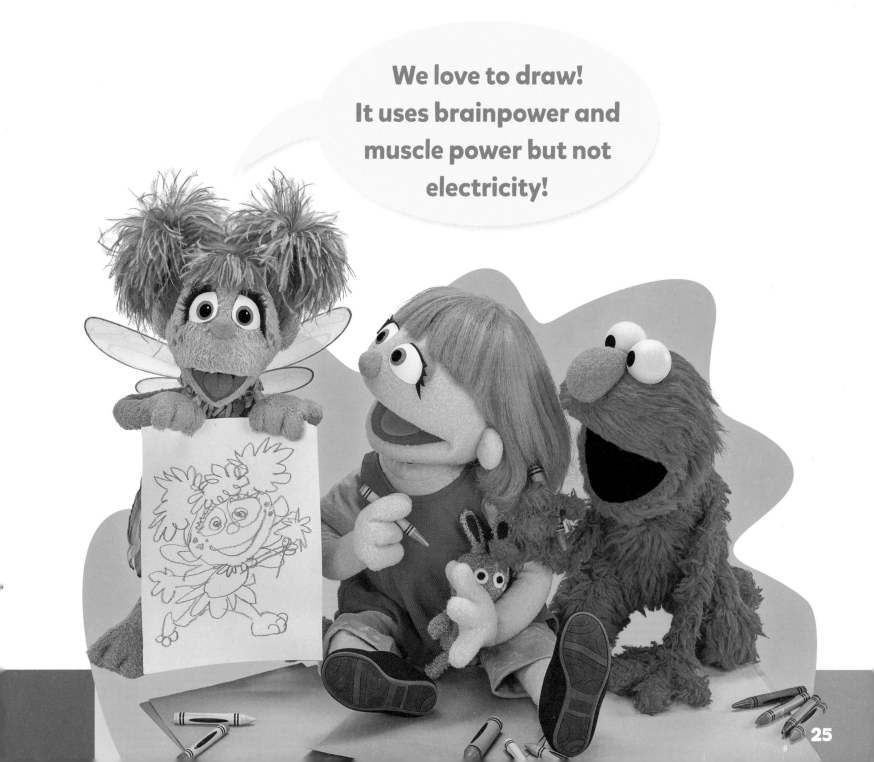

Making small changes to save energy can make a big difference for the planet.

Earth Day Every Day

Earth Day is April 22. This holiday celebrates how important Earth is to plants, animals, and people.

Let's grow fruit!

People may plant trees and flowers on Earth Day. They may pick up garbage from the land and the water. How would *you* celebrate Earth Day?

Me want to grow cookie flower for Earth Day!

Have a Me-Powered Afternoon

Challenge your family or friends to a me-powered afternoon. No electricity needed!

1. Plan activities that don't use electricity. You could explore a playground, play a board game, take a walk, or so much more!

2. Invite your family or friends to join in.

3. Think about your afternoon. What was the most fun? What could you do next time?

Glossary

electricity: a form of energy. Electricity powers many things, such as lights and TVs.

panels: a flat surface. Solar panels collect sunlight for energy.

solar energy: energy from the sun

turbine: a machine that makes electricity when wind spins its blades

Index

carpool, 22

electricity, 11, 16, 24–25

lights, 6, 20–21

power, 10, 25

solar energy, 14–15

travel, 9

wind energy, 16

Photo Acknowledgments

Additional image credits: Vector Icon Flat/Shutterstock.com (throughout); Westend61/Getty Images, p. 5; evgenyatamanenko/Getty Images, p. 6; JGalione/Getty Images, p. 7; Hero Images/Getty Images, p. 8; Greg Bajor/Getty Images, p. 9; Rawpixel.com/Shutterstock.com, p. 10; aanbetta/Shutterstock.com, p. 11 (TV); Flashpop/Getty Images, p. 11 (singer); tibu/Getty Images, p. 12; Karel Bock/Shutterstock.com, p. 13; rangizzz/Shutterstock.com, p. 14; deepblue4you/Getty Images, p. 15; photographer/agency/Getty Images, p. 17; Keith Stewart/500px/Getty Images, p. 18; Golden Pixels LLC/Shutterstock.com, p. 19; Imgorthand/Getty Images, p. 20; Ariel Skelley/Getty Images, p. 22; Jose Luis Pelaez Inc/Getty Images, pp. 23, 28; Steve Debenport/Getty Images, p. 24; Ariel Skelley/Getty Images, p. 26; Mireya Acierto/Getty Images, p. 30.
Cover: Somchai Som/Shutterstock.com (light bulb); vectortatu/Shutterstock.com (background).

Lerner Publications Company
An imprint of Lerner Publishing Group, Inc.
241 First Avenue North
Minneapolis, MN 55401 USA

For reading levels and more information, look up this title at www.lernerbooks.com.

Main body text set in Mikado.
Typeface provided by HVD.

Library of Congress Cataloging-in-Publication Data

Title: Save energy, Bert and Ernie! / Jennifer Boothroyd.
Other titles: Sesame Street (Television program)
Description: Minneapolis : Lerner Publications, [2020] | Series: Go green with Sesame Street | Audience: Ages: 4–8. | Audience: Grades: K to Grade 3. | Includes bibliographical references and index.
Identifiers: LCCN 2019012420 (print) | LCCN 2019018587 (ebook) | ISBN 9781541583139 (eb pdf) | ISBN 9781541572577 (library binding : alk. paper)
Subjects: LCSH: Energy conservation—Juvenile literature. | Environmentalism—Juvenile literature. | Earth Day—Juvenile literature.
Classification: LCC TJ163.35 (ebook) | LCC TJ163.35 .B66 2020 (print) | DDC 333.79/16—dc23

LC record available at https://lccn.loc.gov/2019012420

Manufactured in the United States of America
1-46524-47569-6/20/2019